CANADA GEESE

by Matt Lilley

Cody Koala

An Imprint of Pop!
popbooksonline.com

abdobooks.com
Published by Pop!, a division of ABDO, PO Box 398166, Minneapolis,
Minnesota 55439. Copyright © 2019 by POP, LLC. International copyrights
reserved in all countries. No part of this book may be reproduced in any
form without written permission from the publisher. Pop!™ is a trademark
and logo of POP, LLC.

Printed in the United States of America, North Mankato, Minnesota

092018
012019

**THIS BOOK CONTAINS
RECYCLED MATERIALS**

Cover Photo: iStockphoto
Interior Photos: iStockphoto, 1, 5 (top), 13; Shutterstock Images,
5 (bottom left), 5 (bottom right), 6, 9, 10, 11, 15, 16, 19 (top),
19 (bottom left), 19 (bottom right), 21

Editor: Charly Haley
Series Designer: Laura Mitchell

Library of Congress Control Number: 2018950113

Publisher's Cataloging-in-Publication Data

Names: Lilley, Matt, author.
Title: Canada Geese / by Matt Lilley.
Description: Minneapolis, Minnesota: Pop!, 2019 | Series: Pond animals |
    Includes online resources and index.
Identifiers: ISBN 9781532162053 (lib. bdg.) | ISBN 9781641855761 (pbk) |
    ISBN 9781532163111 (ebook)
Subjects: LCSH: Canadian goose--Juvenile literature. | Birds--Behavior--
    Juvenile literature. | Pond animals--Juvenile literature.
Classification: DDC 598.4178--dc23

Hello! My name is

Cody Koala

Pop open this book and you'll find QR codes like this one, loaded with information, so you can learn even more!

Scan this code* and others like it while you read, or visit the website below to make this book pop.

popbooksonline.com/canada-geese

*Scanning QR codes requires a web-enabled smart device with a QR code reader app and a camera.

Table of Contents

Chapter 1

Canada Geese

Canada geese are big birds with long necks. Their heads and necks are black. Each goose has a white patch on its throat.

Watch a video here!

Canada geese float in water. They swim with their webbed feet. They stick their heads in the water and eat plants.

Canada geese have sharp beaks for grabbing food. They eat berries, seeds, grass, and underwater plants.

Geese fly together as a **flock.**

Canada geese **graze** in open fields. In fields, they can see far away. They can see any **predators** nearby.

Geese honk to warn other geese about predators. Then they fly away.

Migration

Canada geese live in the United States, Canada, and part of Mexico. In the fall, geese **migrate** south for warm winter weather. In the spring, they fly back north.

Learn more here!

Nesting

Canada geese make their nests near water. Female geese sit on their eggs in the nests.

Learn more here!

A male goose is called a **gander**. He stays near the nest, guarding the eggs and the female goose. If anyone comes too close, he hisses.

Goslings

Young geese are called **goslings**. Their fluffy feathers are yellow and brown.

Complete an activity here!

Within hours of hatching, goslings are ready for their first swim. When they are about two months old, the goslings learn to fly.

Young geese stay with their parents for about a year.

Making Connections

Text-to-Self

Have you ever seen a Canada goose? If not, have you seen another animal in the wild?

Text-to-Text

Have you read another book about a different animal? How is that animal similar to a Canada goose? How is it different?

Text-to-World

Geese migrate when the seasons change. They fly north in the spring and south in the fall. What else happens when the seasons change?

Glossary

flock – a group of birds.

gander – a male goose.

gosling – a young goose.

graze – to eat grass in a field.

migrate – to move from one place to another when the seasons change.

predator – an animal that hunts and eats other animals.

Index

Online Resources

popbooksonline.com

Thanks for reading this Cody Koala book!

Scan this code* and others like it in this book, or visit the website below to make this book pop!

popbooksonline.com/canada-geese

*Scanning QR codes requires a web-enabled smart device with a QR code reader app and a camera.